D1609362

BIOKIT

BIOKIT

A JOURNEY TO LIFE

Text and illustrations by
Joël de Rosnay

Drawn by:
Puig Rosado

BIOKIT IS A REGISTERED TRADEMARK OF
CAROLINA BIOLOGICAL SUPPLY COMPANY,
BURLINGTON, NC 27215 (919) 584–0381

 orgenics ltd. ADAMA BOOKS, NEW YORK

THE SECRET OF LIFE:
Information and How it Is Communicated

Hi! I'm Protix (a simple protein molecule). I'm going to be your guide during this voyage through the infinitely minute.

It's easy to see that all living things of the same species resemble one another. Turtles look like turtles, butterflies like butterflies, giraffes like giraffes, and children like their parents.

This is because nature operates according to a **manufacturing plan** which is transmitted from generation to generation. This plan assures
1. The reproduction of a living organism.
2. The control of its vital functions.

Of course you already know that this mysterious plan is DNA, the long nucleic acid molecule that carries hereditary characteristics.

Patience, I'll explain what DNA means later. But you can already tell that the NA part is nucleic acid.

Without DNA, living organisms – microbes, animals and plants – could neither reproduce themselves, nor permanently control the billions of chemical reactions which keep their cells alive and make the products they need.

DNA is information stored at the level of molecules (a millionth of a millimeter!)

The mechanisms by which information is exchanged **in** the living cell and **between** cells constitute the basis for cellular communication. Without cellular communication life would not be possible.

I'm sure you know that without communication human society could not exist. The living organism can be thought of as a society – **a society of cells** that communicate with each other. (There are probably 60,000 billion of them in your body, not counting germs and other small creatures that live there.)

Human society

The body:
a society of cells

The cell:
a society of molecules

But in what form does this information circulate between the molecules and between the cells?

In our society, information is transported by words or phrases of written or spoken language, by sounds and symbols. The transport mechanisms are very diverse and complicated. They range from the simple, such as air vibrations or signs on paper, to the complicated and sophisticated, such as the telephone, the newspaper, radio, television and films...and road signs. Information that is electronically coded is transmitted between computers.

The cell itself, visible only through a microscope (it's the smallest organized structure in the living world), is in itself a **society of molecules** that are constantly exchanging information. In the organism, the cells communicate at a distance by means of the nervous and hormonal systems. Hormones are molecules made by specialized cells, and transported by the circulation of the blood. These are the "signals" capable of triggering a specific action in an organ whose cells have the appropriate receptors.

Life is thus a coded language: The letters, words and phrases that make up this code are the **molecules** that transport and store biological information. These molecules may be very long, like DNA or proteins, or very short like hormones.

Dissection of the Structures of Life

Hey! I'm already telling you about DNA, proteins, and big and little molecules... Let's take a short break to understand where all this puts us.

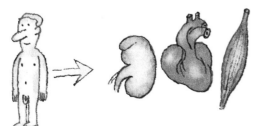

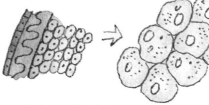

1 The body is made of **organs**, muscles, blood vessels, bone, etc.

2 Each organ or muscle is made of **tissue**, and the tissue is made of **cells**.

3 In the cells we find organized **structures** such as the nucleus, membrane, mitochondria, ribosomes, vacuoles, microtubules, etc.

This is me here!

4 These structures are made of **proteins, nucleic acids** and other gigantic molecules (macromolecules), polysaccharides (sugars), fats, etc.

5 Proteins, nucleic acids, polysaccharides, etc., are all made of **smaller molecules** attached one to the other in linear chains, or in complex structures.

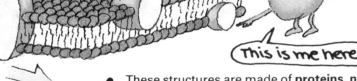

6 These molecules are made of **atoms**, a combination of carbon (C), hydrogen (H), oxygen (O), nitrogen (N), sulfur (S) and phosphorous (P).

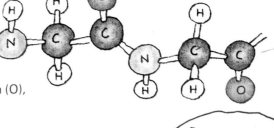

On what level does this fantastic construction take place?

7 At every level of construction, elements are combined to form new structures that become the elements of the next level: **atoms** in the molecule, **molecules** in the **macromolecule**, which in turn form **organized cellular structures**, which combine to form cells, the **cells** in the tissue, the **tissue** in the organs, the **organs** in the organism, the **organisms** in the populations, the **populations** in the societies, and the **societies** on the entire planet.

A SUPER MICROSCOPE FOR LOOKING AT MOLECULES

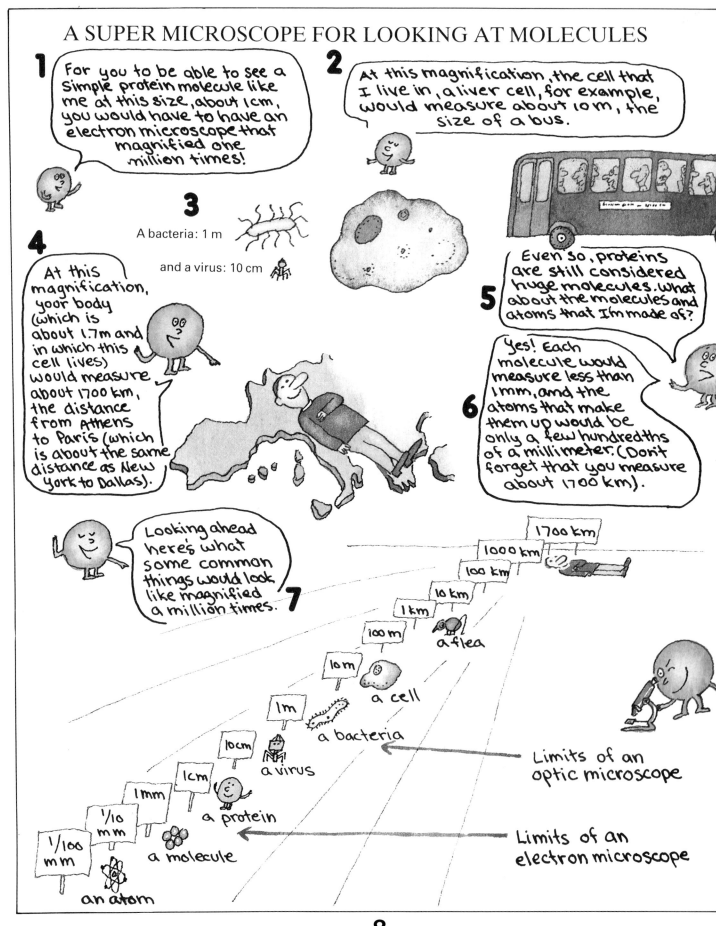

1 For you to be able to see a simple protein molecule like me at this size, about 1cm, you would have to have an electron microscope that magnified one million times!

2 At this magnification, the cell that I live in, a liver cell, for example, would measure about 10 m, the size of a bus.

3 A bacteria: 1 m

and a virus: 10 cm

4 At this magnification, your body (which is about 1.7m and in which this cell lives) would measure about 1700 km, the distance from Athens to Paris (which is about the same distance as New York to Dallas).

5 Even so, proteins are still considered huge molecules. What about the molecules and atoms that I'm made of?

6 Yes! Each molecule would measure less than 1mm, and the atoms that make them up would be only a few hundredths of a millimeter. (Don't forget that you measure about 1700 km).

7 Looking ahead here's what some common things would look like magnified a million times.

1700 km
1000 km
100 km
10 km
1 km
100 m
a flea
10 m
a cell
1m
a bacteria
10cm
a virus
1cm
a protein
1mm
1/10 mm
a molecule
1/100 mm
an atom

Limits of an optic microscope

Limits of an electron microscope

8

The Letters, Words and Phrases of Life

The language that allows communication in and between the cells is a coded language whose letters, words and phrases are molecules or collections of molecules. But look! Each family of molecules, small or large, has a particular form (like letters of the alphabet or like a key).

Here are the real forms of some common molecules, magnified 100 million times. (Imagine that you are measuring the distance between the earth and the moon.) Each is similar to a key: It carries information that is indigenous to its structure. This information can be retrieved by other molecules that have the complementary form. It's the same as a key that opens only one lock.

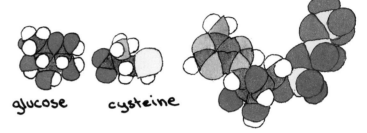

glucose   cysteine

ATP adenosine triphosphate, universal fuel for all living organisms.

you can see that the key is simultaneously the message and the messenger who carries the information.

KEY

LOCK

Signal
↓
receptor

The lock is the memory that stores information as well as the system of recognition that can trigger a reaction.

Since certain molecules (like hormones) are **at the same time** the messenger and the message they're transporting, there is system for coding, storing, and transmitting information. The receptors can then recover the information and trigger the appropriate action. Probably one of the secrets of biological communication and of the language of life exists in these molecules.

Throughout this network of communications, proteins occupy a privileged position. Admittedly they often play a passive role, as bricks or building materials for the cell. But when they make, transform, or recognize other molecules, they play an active role. Some proteins are enzymes that perform precise functions. They are the machine tools or indefatigable chemists of the cells. Other proteins are antibodies which protect us against invaders (germs and viruses).

Enzymes make all the molecules that serve cellular life (obviously also themselves and those that transport information). But what gives the enzymes the ability to control all the reactions of living cells? What teaches them to do this job? How do they get their function?

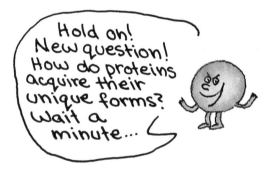

PROTEINS: The Building Blocks and Machinery of the Cell Factory

a protein that kills
(such as snake venom)

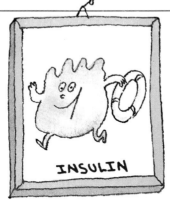

a protein that saves lives

a protein that defends us
against germs

a protein that is needed to make
skin, bone and connective tissue

a protein that cleans the blood

a protein that eats
other proteins

a protein that breathes oxygen

a protein that nourishes us

Proteins are the principal constituents of all living organisms: microbes, animals and plants. There are probably 5,000 different families of proteins in an animal or plant cell. Each protein has a special role.

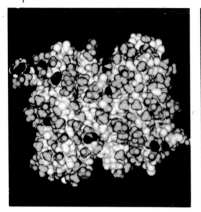
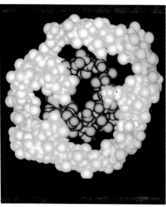
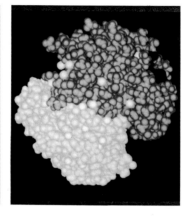
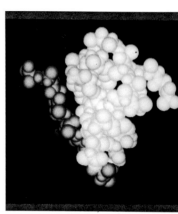

Cytochrome   Triose Phosphate Isomerase   Hemoglobin   Insulin

Here is what several proteins look like. (These pictures of protein molecules were drawn by computer.) Each colored bead is a molecule. The total magnification is 10 million – at that magnification you would be 17,000 km tall. You can see that proteins have very different shapes, and yet they share a common property, that is, their shape is determined by the sequence of elementary building blocks (the molecules of amino acids) that are attached to each other in a well-defined order for each family of proteins.

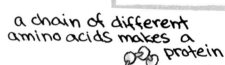

ORDER
sequence of amino acids

SHAPE
form of the protein

FUNCTION

RECOGNITION
MEMORY (STORAGE)
OPERATION
CHARACTERISTICS

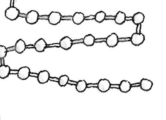

a chain of amino acids

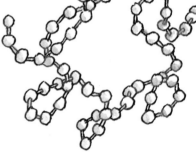

a chain of different amino acids makes a protein

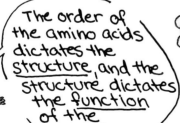

The order of the amino acids dictates the <u>structure</u>, and the structure dictates the <u>function</u> of the protein.

The chain of amino acids makes a structure in one dimension, but as it twists up in space it becomes a three-dimensional structure which determines the molecule's biological activity.

A protein's shape depends largely on the characteristics of certain amino acids that cause

 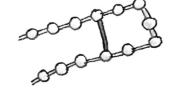 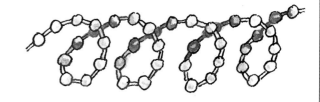

elbows in the chain   **bridges** between two sections of the chain   or twists in the form of a **spiral**.

A good example is the assembling of a track layout for an electric train:

With 6 curved rails, A; 4 straight rails, B; 6 half-sized straight rails; 6 half-sized curved rails; and one crossing, you can make many different track layouts, provided you have a plan for the layout.

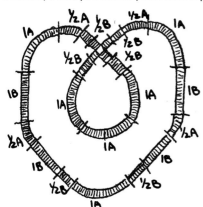 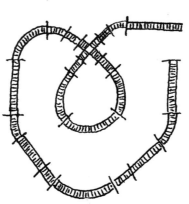

If you use 5 curves instead of 6, or if you replace a curved rail by a straight one, then everything will change. The rest of the track might not reach the crossing or the track might not close.

It's easy to see that if the amino acids that make "elbows," or "crossings" or "spirals" are not in their proper places, the shape of the protein is all mixed up.

It's me! Protix! There must have been a slight error in assembly...!

Like the rails in the toy train set, the order of succession of the amino acids in a protein is essential.
But who are these amino acids whose role is so crucial in determining all the reactions of life?
There are twenty sorts of amino acids in proteins. Simply by changing the order of the twenty building blocks, the cells make thousands of different proteins, just as one can, using the twenty-six letters of the alphabet, write anything from poems to patents to recipes.

Here's a list of the twenty amino acids found in proteins

Name	Abbr.	Name	Abbr.	Name	Abbr.	Name	Abbr.
Alanine	Ala	Glycine	Gly	Methionine	Met	Serine	Ser
Cysteine	Cys	Histidine	His	Asparagine	Asn	Threonine	Thr
Aspartic acid	Asp	Isoleucine	Ile	Proline	Pro	Valine	Val
Glumatic acid	Glu	Lysine	Lys	Glutamine	Gln	Tryptophan	Trp
Phenylalanine	Phe	Leucine	Leu	Arginine	Arg	Tyrosine	Tyr

An amino acid is a small molecule with a system of "standard chemical linkages," or characteristics which render it comparable to a sort of chemical "tool." A chain of several amino acids is called a **peptide**. A neuro-peptide (a recently discovered hormone of the brain) for example, is made of the amino acids Try-Gly-Gly-Phe-Met. Another peptide, a little bit longer, discovered by Nobel-Prize-winner Roger Guillemin, is somatostatin: Ala-Gly-Cys-Lys-Asn-Phe-Phe-Tyr-Lys-Tyr-Phe-Tyr-Ser-Cys.

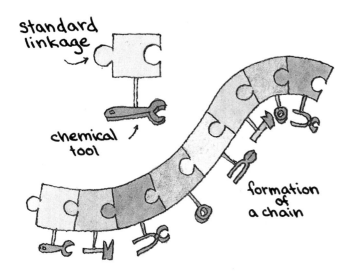

standard linkage

chemical tool

formation of a chain

A small protein has perhaps 30–100 amino acids, a medium sized protein 100–300, and a very large protein, like albumin, 585. A huge protein, such as collagen,* has 1052! You can imagine just how many combinations you can get by placing 1052 amino acids in different orders!

* The most abundant protein in mammals, collagen is in skin, bones, tendons, cartilage, blood vessels, teeth, etc.

Today, the computer allows us to compare the sequences of amino acids in proteins and find similarities in protein families.

Here's how the bending and twisting of the flexible amino acid chain carrying its chemical tools gives biological activity to an enzyme, gives it its power of chemical transformation and its ability to regulate cellular reactions.

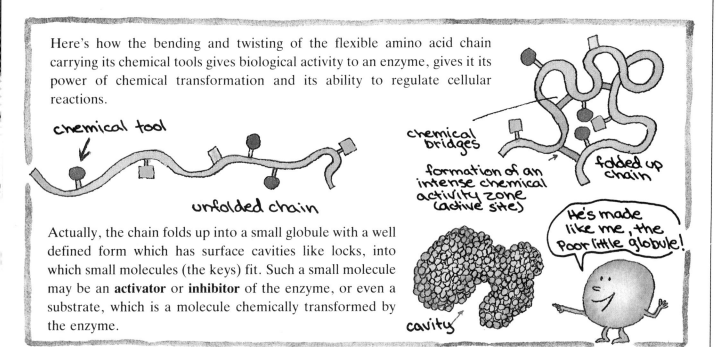

chemical tool

unfolded chain

chemical bridges

formation of an intense chemical activity zone (active site)

folded up chain

cavity

He's made like me, the poor little globule!

Actually, the chain folds up into a small globule with a well defined form which has surface cavities like locks, into which small molecules (the keys) fit. Such a small molecule may be an **activator** or **inhibitor** of the enzyme, or even a substrate, which is a molecule chemically transformed by the enzyme.

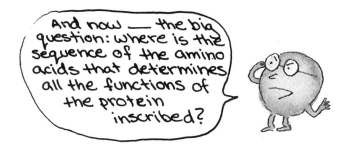

And now — the big question: where is the sequence of the amino acids that determines all the functions of the protein inscribed?

When we write a text, the order of the letters, words, sentences, paragraphs, chapters, etc., is dictated by the rules of syntax and grammar, and by the information we possess about the subject.

Coded information that we find inscribed in the order of amino acids is carried by a single family of macromolecules, the **nucleic acids**, the bearers of hereditary characteristics.

We call these molecules nucleic acids because they were first discovered in the nuclei of cells.

DNA:
Cellular Programming

DNA is a long spiral molecule in the nucleus of the cell, usually in the form of chromosomes, or freely coiled in the bacterial cell, which has no nucleus.

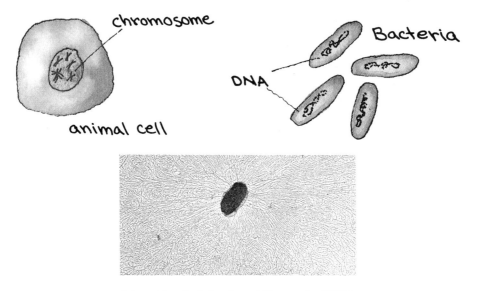

A burst bacterial cell and filament of DNA

If you uncoiled all the DNA in one human cell, the filament (invisible to the human eye) would measure about 1.5 m. The DNA of all the cells in the body, stretched end to end, would form a filament that stretched from the earth to the moon.

With the million power magnification used on p. 8, your body measured 1700 km. At that magnification, the DNA of one single cell would have a length of approximately 1500 km and a width of only 3 mm!

DNA coils upon itself many times, and has a complex structure of "braided" or "woven" cables linked to the proteins, and visible with an ordinary microscope only in the form of little sticks. These are the chromosomes. There are 46 of them in each human cell.

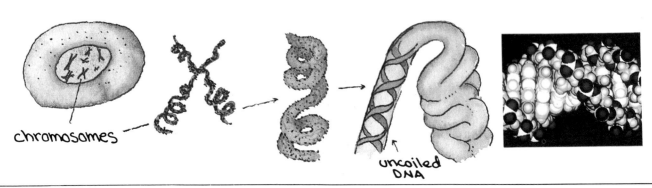

The DNA chain looks like a rope ladder twisted around itself lengthwise. This ladder is made by the association of four different molecules:

a brick called T (for thymine)
a brick called C (for cytosine)
a brick called A (for adenine)
a brick called G (for guanine)

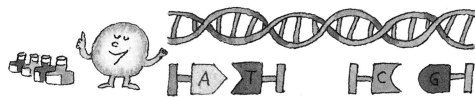

These little bricks are fixed on a section of the ladder which welds them together lengthwise. This system of linkages is standard and identical for the four molecules.* The system is actually made from a sugar molecule, deoxyribose, that acts as a support for the rungs of the ladder, and of another molecule, phosphoric acid, that makes the lengthwise connections. Thanks to the sugar molecule deoxyribose, DNA has the horribly long, complicated name, deoxyribonucleic acid.

* This system of linkage is represented here by:

The bricks T, C, A and G can therefore attach themselves one to the other to form a half of the ladder.

These bricks pair up laterally, making the rungs of the ladder. The pairs have complementary structures, shown here by light blue and dark blue for A and T, and by pink and red for C and G.
It's because of this association that they can make up the rungs and the two sides of the ladder that coils itself up to form the famous double helix.

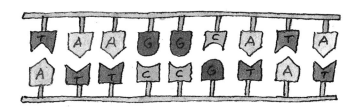

As a result of its particular structure, the DNA molecule has two principal properties:

1 It can divide itself in two lengthwise, making two complementary chains. That's how the master plan of creation is copied and transmitted from generation to generation.

2 It contains the instructions that determine the exact sequence of amino acids in proteins, as well as the regulatory systems that control the synthesis of proteins: more proteins, less proteins, faster, slower.

The DNA molecule is the chemical carrier of genes. A gene is a sequence of nucleotides of the DNA molecule that contains the instructions for making a given protein. The DNA molecule is a veritable ultraminiaturized program, made of a succession of letters: the four bricks T,C,A and G.

For example: here's the beginning of the genetic code for the protein hormone for human growth:

TTC CCA ACT ATA CCA CTA TCT CGT CTA TTC...

and for another (human interferon):

ATG GCC TTG ACC TTT GCT TTA CTG GTG GCC...

We call each letter a __base__ and the whole brick a __nucleotide__.

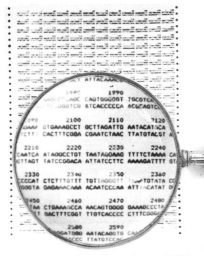

Here is, finally, the whole program of a virus – that of hepatitis B. It contains 3182 letters of genetic code (that's enough to make us very sick).

A gene is made of about one thousand letters (a thousand base pairs).
A bacteria contains about 3000 genes, and that makes a program of about 3 million letters.
A human cell contains 500 to 1000 times as many genes as a bacteria. The program for a human being contains about 3 billion letters.

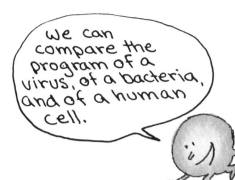

THE PROGRAM OF A VIRUS	THE PROGRAM OF A MICROBE	THE PROGRAM OF A CELL
DNA OF A VIRUS	**DNA OF A BACTERIA**	**DNA OF A HUMAN CELL**
(it's circular)	(spreading in all directions)	(contained in the chromosomes)

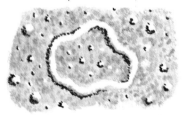

Hepatitis B

3182 letters of
genetic code
is

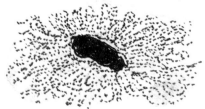

Escherichia Coli

3 million letters of
genetic code
is

3 billion letters
of genetic code
is

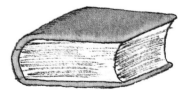

one page of 3000 characters
at 100 characters per line
and 30 lines per page.

an encyclopedia of 1000 pages,
with 3000 characters per page
(about 5 cm thick).

1000 encyclopedias 5 cm thick piled one
on top of another, about 50 m high,
about as tall as a twenty story building.

DIVISION OF DNA: Two Identical Copies

The first fundamental property of DNA is that it gives identical copies by opening into two single strands (thanks to the enzymes).

Here's the original.

The two strands separate like a zipper, thanks again to the enzymes.

Since there is a profusion of bricks A,T,G and C in the environment and each strand preserves the order of the letters, the newly created strands also preserve the order of the letters of the code.

Here are the two finished copies. The separation of the old, and the linking of the new strands occur at a rate of 10–20 nucleotides per second.

In reality, the enzymes uncoil the double helix and make two new chains.

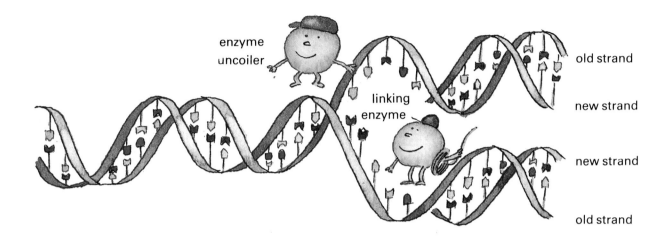

enzyme
uncoiler

linking
enzyme

old strand

new strand

new strand

old strand

The Secret Code of Life

The second fundamental property of DNA is that it stocks the coded instructions necessary for specifying the order of amino acids in proteins. The major problem in the transmission of biological information is transcribing it and then translating it from the language of DNA to the language of proteins.

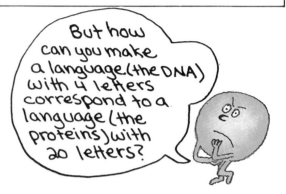

What method of decoding would be best suited for this translation? What dictionary to use? What translating machine would work effectively? The succession of four letters, the long part of the double helix, forms the basis of the code, but with only four letters (A,T,G, and C) we can only code four amino acids (not twenty!). What can we do?

Imagine, for example, that

T is a code for tyr
C is a code for cys
A is a code for ala
G is a code for glu

Which is evidently false, but helps for purposes of explaining.

The coded message could be:

The clear translation is: ALA TYR GLU CYS GLU TYR ALA TYR TYR ALA

The problem is, we only used four amino acids of the twenty available. It just doesn't work!

I've got an idea! If we combine the letters of the code two by two that should give...

TT CT AT GT

TC CC AC GC

TA CA AA GA

TG CG AG GG

Terrific! That gives 64 combinations of three letters (codons), which is enough to code twenty amino acids.

Here's what that gives:

TTT	CTT	ATT	GTT
TTC	CTC	ATC	GTC
TTA	CTA	ATA	GTA
TTG	CTG	ATG	GTG
TCT	CCT	ACT	GCT
TCC	CCC	ACC	GCC
TCA	CCA	ACA	GCA
TCG	CCG	ACG	GCG
TAT	CAT	AAT	GAT
TAC	CAC	AAC	GAC
TAA	CAA	AAA	GAA
TAG	CAG	AAG	GAG
TGT	CGT	AGT	GGT
TGC	CGC	AGC	GGC
TGA	CGA	AGA	GGA
TGG	CGG	AGG	GGG

Nope! That only makes 16 combinations, and there are twenty amino acids...

Wait! maybe if we combine them three by three...

Today, researchers have succeeded in decoding the genetic code. The genetic code is the same for all living things, from the microbe to the whale, from the flower to the tree, and to man.... For each group of letters, there is a corresponding amino acid, or an indication of something else. (STOP, for example, indicates the stopping of the translating machine.) Since there are 64 groups of three letters, and only twenty amino acids, several groups of three letters designate the **same** amino acid, that's for sure!

1st position	2nd position				3rd position
	T	C	A	G	
T	Phe	Ser	Tyr	Cys	T
	Phe	Ser	Tyr	Cys	C
	Leu	Ser	Stop	Stop	A
	Leu	Ser	Stop		G
C	Leu	Pro	His	Arg	T
	Leu	Pro	His	Arg	C
	Leu	Pro	Glu	Arg	A
	Leu	Pro	Glu	Arg	G
A	Ile	Thr	Asp	Ser	T
	Ile	Thr	Asp	Ser	C
	Ile	Thr	Lys	Arg	A
	Met	Thr	Lys	Arg	G
G	Val	Ala	Asp	Gly	T
	Val	Ala	Asp	Gly	C
	Val	Ala	Glu	Gly	A
	Val	Ala	Glu	Gly	G

Amino acids

For example, the codes CAT and CAC designate histidine, whereas valine is represented by GGT, GTC, GTA and GTG.

The Synthesis of Proteins

The transcription and translation of the language of DNA is now possible. To do this, the cell uses a system based on two machines: a machine to copy the DNA, the enzyme RNA polymerase, and a machine to translate the DNA into protein language.

The machine to copy DNA

DNA itself is too precious to intervene directly in the translating machines: If it were damaged, the errors would be transmitted from generation to generation. (Sometimes this happens anyway, as we will see on p. 41). Because of this, the translating machines use copies of the genes.

The copies are made from another form of nucleic acid, RNA (ribonucleic acid). It differs from DNA in three major ways:

1. It is made of a single strand.
2. The support (sugar) is made of ribose (instead of deoxyribose).
3. The letter U (uracil) replaces the letter T (thymine), as the letter that combines with A.

These copies are called messenger RNA, because they transport the code of the DNA to the translating machine.

The machine for translating the DNA into proteins

The translating machines (ribosomes) work in a chain one behind the other while they read the message of the DNA transcribed in the messenger RNA.

I'm a ribosome!

He's five times bigger than I am, and weighs 100 times as much.

Ribosome 5   Ribosome 4   Ribosome 3   Ribosome 2   Ribosome 1

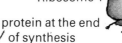

I'm finished!

protein at the end of synthesis

completed protein

It's me, Protix!

messenger RNA (genetic code)

But an essential final piece is still needed in the translating mechanism: an **adapter-decoder**. It links the language of the messenger RNA and that of the protein in synthesis, and it assures exact placement of each amino acid. This adapter has an anticodon at one end in contact with the messenger RNA and, at the other end, the corresponding amino acid which it always carries.

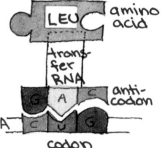

This universal adapter is called transfer RNA. It carries at one end the amino acid and at the other end the anti-codon that recognizes the complementary codon on the messenger RNA (this may appear to be a little complicated, but you'll understand everything with the help of the Biokit).

There exists in the cell as many different kinds of transfer RNA as there are codons for amino acids. In order for these amino acids to be connected to form a protein, they have to be placed a good distance from each other and in the proper order for the given protein.

The transfer RNA (adapter, decoder) uses a very simple system for this. It recognizes its place on the messenger RNA by regrouping locally a double-strand with the messenger RNA (it is the interaction of the codon-anticodon).

It is thus impossible for transfer RNA carrying histidine, for example (anticodon GUG, codon CAC), to place itself on a code other than CAC.

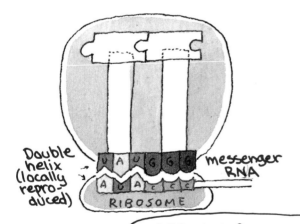

It's because of this that the amino acids are connected in the proper order. Each amino acid is perfectly positioned in the translating machine by the transfer RNA that carries it.

The ribosome is the basis of the assembly mechanisms. It provides two places for two transfer RNAs, permits the transport of energy to make the machine work, assembles the growing protein chain, and finally, makes it all advance by the movement of a trammel-like thing, like the play head on a tape recorder.

You can see, for example, that if it tries to combine with codon GAG the linkage doesn't take place. It's impossible for an amino acid to interlock at the wrong place.

The assembly mechanism of translation

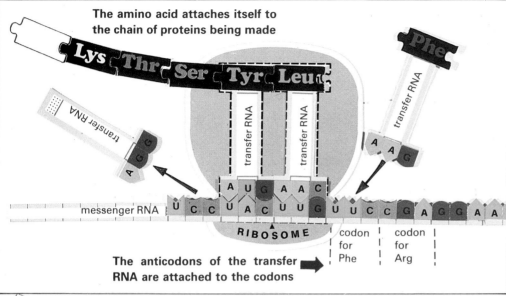

The amino acid attaches itself to the chain of proteins being made

The anticodons of the transfer RNA are attached to the codons ➡

1 Here's the mechanism of translation that you can recreate with the Biokit. Two transfer RNAs find their place on the ribosome. The anticodons form a local double strand with the codons. The link is established between the two amino acids. We see the transfer RNA which carries the amino acid **Phe** arriving from the right. Its anticodon AAG moves into place on the codon UUC.

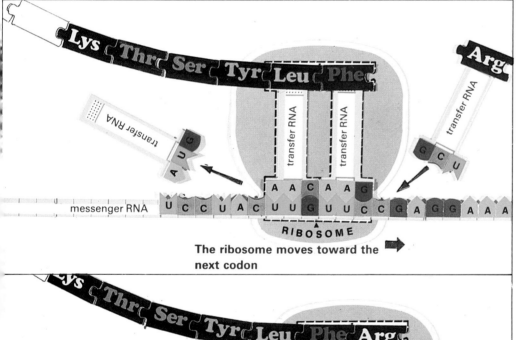

The ribosome moves toward the next codon

2 The ribosome moves on to the next codon. The transfer RNA which had carried the amino acid **Tyr** (anticodon AUG, codon UAC) detaches itself, and the link between **Leu** and **Phe** is made, and **Arg** (anticodon GCU, codon CGA) moves into place from the transfer RNA on the right.

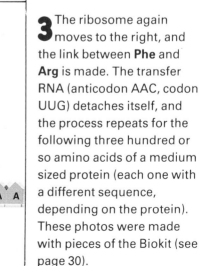

The ribosome "reads" the next codon

3 The ribosome again moves to the right, and the link between **Phe** and **Arg** is made. The transfer RNA (anticodon AAC, codon UUG) detaches itself, and the process repeats for the following three hundred or so amino acids of a medium sized protein (each one with a different sequence, depending on the protein). These photos were made with pieces of the Biokit (see page 30).

How were DNA and protein molecules discovered? Why are they so important in the history of modern biology? Their discoveries can be compared to the invention of the printing press in importance and impact.

In what order were these prodigious discoveries made? This shortened history should give you some idea.

From Mendel to the machine for synthesizing genes

1860 The Austrian monk Gregor Mendel proves that transmission of hereditary characteristics obeys precise rules. This is the birth of the idea of genes.

1920 The American Thomas Hunt Morgan demonstrates that genes are on the chromosomes found in the nuclei of cells.

1940 The American Oswald Avery irrefutably demonstrates that genes are made of molecules of nucleic acid, DNA.

1953 The American J. Watson and the Englishman F.H. Crick propose the structure of DNA. It's a double helix that contains genetic information in coded form.

1961 The Frenchmen Jacques Monod and Francois Jacob suggest a regulatory mechanism for the synthesis of proteins.

1965 The Englishman Frederick Sanger cuts up proteins and analyzes the order of amino acids. Edman elaborates the sequencer. It's the first machine to read the code of life.

1977 A.M. Maxam and W.A. Gilbert develop a quick method of reading the letters of the genetic code. The way is clear for a machine to read genes automatically.

1978 S. Cohen and H. Boyer succeed in the first reprogramming of a living organism, thanks to genetic engineering, and produce a hormone, somatostatine.

1981 Itakura and Leroy Hood develop an automatic machine to synthesize genes. It's the first machine to actually write the code of life....

But there are still some really good mysteries in biology. One of the biggest revolves around what you've just seen: The biological information is contained in a linear form of DNA and the proteins. But how, with information in **one dimension**, can **three-dimensional** organisms, such as an elephant, a dog, a bee, a robin, an ant, or a human brain (that tries, with much pain, to understand how this can go on), be constructed? There is still grist for the biologists' mill!

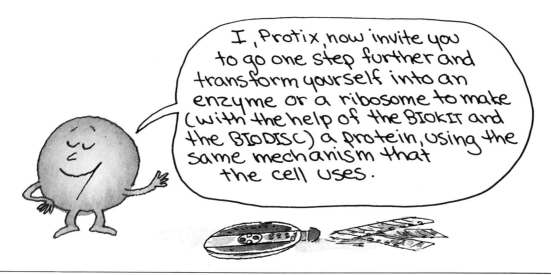

I, Protix, now invite you to go one step further and transform yourself into an enzyme or a ribosome to make (with the help of the BIOKIT and the BIODISC) a protein, using the same mechanism that the cell uses.

I now present to you...

THE BIOKIT

The Biokit is a didactic tool that allows the user to understand how proteins are made in the cell with the genetic information contained in the DNA. With the help of the Biokit, you'll see how the different pieces come together and arrange themselves to allow the making of the fundamental constituents of the cell: proteins.

you're going to play the role of the enzymes, the messenger RNA, the ribosome, and the transfer RNA.

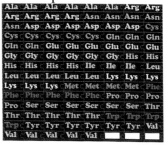

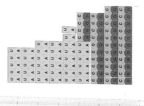

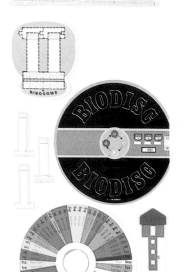

The Biokit is made up of cardboard game pieces in a plastic bag attached to the inside back cover of this book. The bag also contains the Biodisc, the chart for deciphering the genetic code, allowing the translation of the language of genes into the language of proteins.

1 112 amino acids. The number of amino acids is determined by the frequency of their appearances in the most common proteins. **There are, for example, six alanines and six glycines, but only four methionines and four tryptophans.** Three blank pieces are provided so you can make your own extra amino acids with a felt pen or pencil if they're missing from a protein that you want to make.

These amino acids have tabs and slots in the front and back, like puzzle pieces, allowing you to attach one to the other easily. These represent the chemical linkage (peptide linkage CO-NH) that holds amino acids together in real proteins.

2 The 144 bases represent elements of the genetic code. These 144 bases are constituted of 36 A (adenine), 36 U (uracil), 36 C (cytosine), and 36 G (guanine), plus blank pieces that you can mark yourself.* The bases are printed on both sides to allow you to make codons and anticodons.

3 Five cardboard strips represent the sides of the ladder (the phosphate ribose chain) onto which you're going to put the bricks forming the messenger RNA.

4 Three molecules of transfer RNA are also provided. They have, at the top, a place to put the amino acid, and at the bottom, a place to fix the three bases that make up the anticodon.

5 One ribosome, a translating machine that allows you to read the message carried on the messenger RNA, and to translate into the language of proteins.

6 Strips of double-sided tape, protected by wax paper, are there to help you attach the different pieces.

7 The Biodisc, **which you are going to put together yourself with the instructions in the box on the next page.**

* You use the messenger RNA instead of the DNA. This is why uracil (U) replaces thymine (T) on the bases.

How to use the Biodisc

How to put the Biodisc together

Your **Biokit** is in the plastic bag at the end of the book. Cut it out with a pair of scissors.

The **Biodisc** is made of two discs and a moving slide. The disc that has **Biodisc** printed on the side goes on top.

The slide is slid in the notches out to the right of the disc.

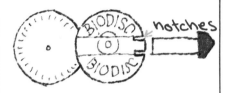

notches

The **second** disc has printed on it (in red and green) the codons and the anti-codons that are going to show through the little windows. Be sure the side with the colored wedges is showing.

Once the slide is in place and the two discs are on top of one another, attach the pieces to one another with the clasp. Make sure the green and red letters appear correctly in the little windows.

The necessary holes for attaching the clasp are punched in the center of the discs, and on the slide. If the little cardboard circles are still in the holes, push them out before inserting the clasp. If you've lost the clasp, you can use a thumbtack stuck into a cork, or anything else you can think of that might work.

Don't worry if the slide is a bit stiff at the start, it will loosen up as you use it.

The Biodisc is the "chart" of the secret message, allowing the translation of the genetic code into the language of proteins. It's just two discs that turn, one on top of the other. On the bottom disc is printed the codons and the anticodons, as well as the amino acids that they correspond to. On the back of this disc are all the amino acids that make up the common proteins.

The slide has windows which can be placed over the amino acid whose code you're looking for, and allows you to read the three bases that make up the codon or the anticodon of the amino acid.

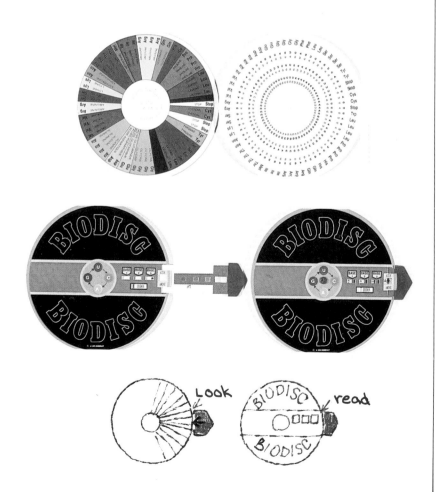

Look

read

Example: You want to look for a genetic code for a given amino acid. Take the disc in your left hand, thumb on top. The side with all the amino acids printed on it should be turned towards you. The arrow allows you to find the amino acid you're looking for very easily. This circle reads counter clockwise. The list of amino acids is therefore read from the bottom up. If an amino acid appears more than once, always take the bottom one, by convention.

When the amino acid is in the right place, turn the disc over, as indicated in the picture. Make sure (in the window at right) that the abbreviation of the amino acid corresponds with that of the one you're looking for. Push the slide to the left if you wish to read a codon, to the right if you wish to read an anticodon. Read base one, base two, and base three in the little windows. Codons should be in green, anticodons in red. Finally, turn over the disc to read the whole amino acid name.*

The Biokit illustrates a number of interesting properties of the genetic code. As you can see, the code is not perfect as there may be **several codons** for the **same** amino acid. Leucine and serine, for example, are coded by six codons each while methionine and tryptophan are each coded by only one codon. For any given amino acid, it's usually only the last letter of the codon that changes while the first two should be constant.

You're going to follow, step by step, the stages of the synthesis of a protein until after several minutes it's completed by the cell. It takes the cell about one minute to make a protein containing one thousand amino acids. This synthesis is done in parallel because many ribosomes at once read the information contained by the messenger RNA (see page 25). All these operations are done **very** precisely, to the hundredth of a micron.

First of all, we have to choose a protein to synthesize. You could choose insulin, or a similar protein, but that has 51 amino acids, and is too big to make with the Biokit.

This is why the demonstration is going to be done with a little peptide, endorphin, a molecule that plays a very important role in the brain, and also with somatostatin, one of the first peptide hormones to be synthesized.

The endorphin sequence is:

Tyr-Gly-Gly-Phe-Met.

The somatostatin sequence is:

Ala-Gly-Cys-Lys-Asn-Phe-Phe-Trp-Lys-Thr-Phe-Thr-Ser-Cys.

* The arrows connecting U, C, A, and G in the center of the top face are to make the search easier by indicating the order of the letters of the code.

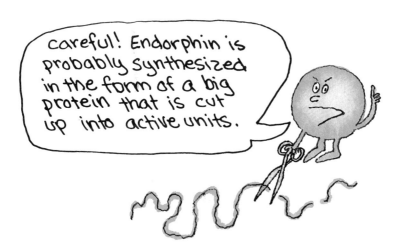

Preparing the pieces

Don't forget that in order to specify the position of one amino acid, you need three bases to form a codon (or anticodon if it's carried by the transfer RNA).

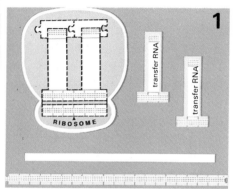

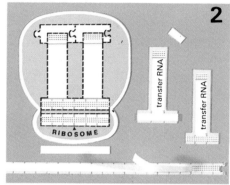

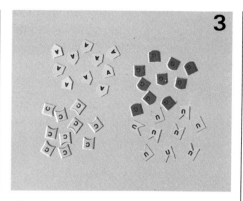

Take the ribosome, two transfer RNAs, a strip of cardboard for a messenger RNA and a strip of double-sided tape (**diagram 1**).
Attach the double-sided tape to the ribosome and transfer RNA (dotted areas).
Cut a strip of double-sided tape for the messenger RNA and stick it on, leaving the paper on the other side

for the moment (**2**).
Detach the precut bases A, U, G and C in advance, and be sure you have enough of them (about 12 of each) (**3**).

Preparation of the messenger RNA

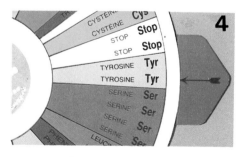

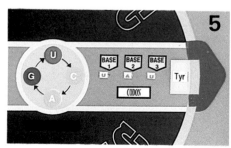

This step is very important, as it's going to determine the code of the protein language.
Take the Biodisc. Now you're going to translate the language of proteins

into the language of the genetic code. To do this, follow the sequence given for endorphine, and note (on a separate piece of paper) the corresponding genetic code. For example, as you

can see, the first amino acid in the sequence is tyrosine (Tyr) (**4**).
With the help of the Biodisc, you can see that the corresponding code is UAU (**5**). Don't forget to take the amino acid lowest on the list.
Continue with the second amino acid, glycine, code GGU. The third amino acid is also glycine, code GGU, etc. The complete genetic code corresponds to a fragment of the messenger RNA code, and therefore: UAUGGUGGUUUUAUG

careful! Line those bases up well!

Transcription of the genetic code

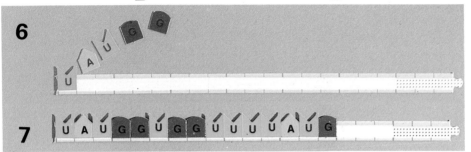

6

7

This step, transcription of the genetic code into the messenger RNA, is done in the cell by the enzyme RNA polymerase.

Take the cardboard strip. It represents a side of the ladder that the phosphate-ribose chain forms (**6**).

Peel the paper off the cardboard strip. Support the strip lightly, and starting at the indicated end, stick on base after base, starting with the three bases that form the first codon (in this case UAU). Be careful to align the bottom of each piece with

the bottom of the tape, so that when the codons face the anticodons there is no mistake.

Continue with the second codon, and be sure to put each base on the indicated place on the cardboard strip (stay between the lines). Continue until you have finished the strip of messenger RNA (**7**).

As you can see, you play the role of the enzyme RNA polymerase that copies the DNA's message into messenger RNA. This copying work is done by the enzyme at the speed of 12–50 nucleotides per second.

Translation of the genetic code into the language of proteins

We're going to translate the secret message, thanks to the ribosome.

1. How to attach the messenger RNA to the ribosome.

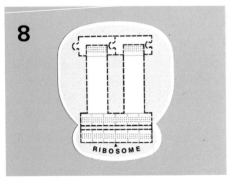

8

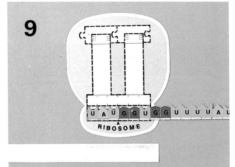

9

Take the ribosome and place it as indicated on **diagram 8**, small end down.

Take the paper off the tape on the ribosome, and attach the indicated

end of the messenger RNA.* Be sure to put the first and second codons in the little boxes, along the thick dotted line on the ribosome with the little arrow separating them (**9**).

This positioning is extremely important. If the position of the messenger RNA is off by one box, the whole thing gets messed up:

In the cell, the ribosome recognizes a signal carried by the messenger RNA, just as in the previous case. At that moment the ribosome attaches itself to the messenger RNA and the translating machinery and the making of proteins begins.

* For the first few times, don't use the tape; it'll make it easier to slide the messenger RNA over the ribosome.

2. Transfer RNA: an adapter-decoder.

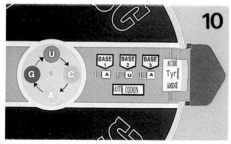

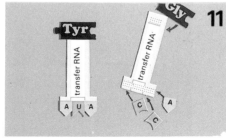

Take the first transfer RNA and assemble the anticodon that it carries on its base. Use the Biodisc to find the anticodon (in red). The anticodon of this particular amino acid, Tyr, is AUA. You can readily see that this is the complementary inverse of UAU (10).

Next, attach the three bases A, U and A to the transfer RNA in the indicated place. Don't forget to turn the bases as indicated in the diagram. (This is easy, as all the bases are printed on both sides.) The "teeth" must be facing down, and the rectangular side of the pieces facing up.

Align them as carefully as you did when you were making your messenger RNA.

Now attach the amino acid tyrosine (Tyr), which is the partner of the first transfer RNA and corresponds to the first anticodon, to the indicated place on the top of the transfer RNA molecule. This attachment is made in the cell by enzymes of the family aminoacyl-t-RNA synthetases, also called activation enzymes.

Your adapter-decoder is now ready to translate the genetic code into the language of proteins (11).

3. Translation of the first codon: Attach the amino acids in the order indicated by the genetic code.

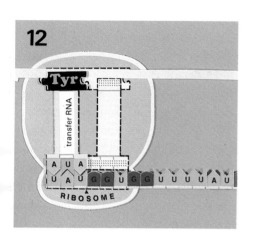

Place the first transfer RNA on the ribosome at the indicated place. You can see that the bases that it carries **fit exactly, with the codon carried by the messenger RNA (12).**

By taking it out and trying other places, you can verify the fact that this anticodon fits only with its corresponding codon, that of the amino acid tyrosine.

Put it back in its place on the ribosome. You can prove that the match between the bases AUA and UAU is locally reconstructed: a double strand or ladder like the double helix of the DNA, but with uracil in the place of thymine, and ribose in the place of deoxyribose.

4. Translation of the second codon: growth of the amino acid chain.

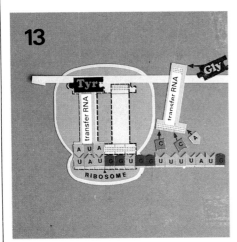

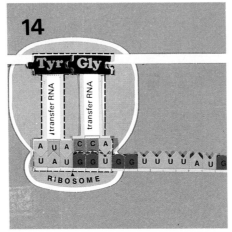

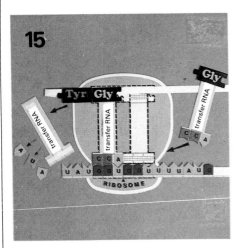

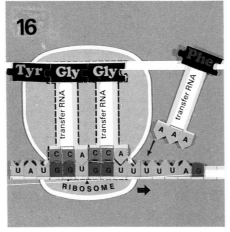

Now take the transfer RNA. As before, find the anticodon for the second amino acid, glycine (Gly). It's CCA (**diagram 13**).

Place the three bases on the transfer RNA, attaching them lightly, as before. Be sure to line up the bases carefully. When you place the second transfer RNA on the ribosome, next to the first tranfer RNA, you'll see that it occupies the only possible place **on the ribosome** for the anticodon that it carries (**14**).

The two amino acids are now next to one another. Complete the linkage yourself by snapping the puzzle piece ends together. You've now made a peptide bond and the protein chain has begun to grow. You can now put a strip of one-sided tape across the amino acids to make them easier to handle.

In the cell, the enzyme peptidyl-transferase performs the attaching reaction.

Note that there are only two places

on the ribosome for molecules of transfer RNA. This is how ribosomes actually are (not made out of cardboard, though).

Also notice that in this particular spot, only glycine can attach itself to tyrosine. **This is how and why the exact order of amino acids in proteins is maintained.** You're going to see this for the amino acids in the chain that you're in the process of making.

5. Displacement of the translating machine for the reading of the next codon.

Pick up the first transfer RNA, but leave the first amino acid, Tyr, attached to the second, Gly, which is still carried by the transfer RNA. Remove the bases of its anticodon. (Save them for later. They're no help to us now. **Diagram 15**.)

Move the ribosome to the right one codon. To do this, unstick the messenger RNA (if it's still stuck) and slide the ribosome to the right a distance of one whole codon (that is, three boxes). Line up the arrow printed on the ribosome with the thick blue line between the second and third codons. This is an essential step. Be sure to keep the pieces in place as you move the ribosome. Transfer RNA no. 2 is also displaced, and is moved to the place previously occupied by transfer RNA no. 1.

6. Translation of the third codon.

Make a new transfer RNA with the anticodon corresponding to amino acid no. 3. (It's glycine again, anticodon CCA. **Diagram 16**.)

In order to attach the amino acid glycine, attach the transfer RNA to the ribosome in place no. 2, next to the transfer RNA in place no. 1.

Make the gly-gly peptide bond. Now you've made a tri-peptide out of three amino acids: Tyr-Gly-Gly. Continue this way to the end of the protein.

There! You've translated letter by letter with the help of the translating machine (the ribosome) and the help of the universal adapter (the transfer RNA) the language of the genetic code into the language of proteins.

Here's the finished endorphine sequence: Tyr-Gly-Gly-Phe-Met and the corresponding sequence in the language of genetic code UAU GGU GGU UUU AUG.

To make your peptide sequence perfect, cut off the ends of the tape.

Now, imagine you're making a chain of 153 amino acids, such as myoglobin. Each amino acid has to be placed in its exact place, according to the genetic code.

This is the **order** that determines the **structure**, and consequently the **function** of the protein.

That's how the cell transforms a piece of information in one dimension into the three dimensional structure that is essential to the reactions of life.

In order to properly understand the mechanisms of protein synthesis, try a peptide that's a bit longer, like somatostatine, with 14 amino acids.

Somatostatin has a very interesting history. It was the first human peptide hormone that was synthesized by genetic engineering. Its role in the organism is an important one. It inhibits the release of the growth hormone by hypophysis, as well as the secretion of insulin and of glycogen. Somatostatin was first isolated in 1972 by Prof. Roger Guillemin of the Salk Institute in California, for which he won the 1980 Nobel Prize for Medicine. Guillemin and his team worked with some 500,000 sheep brains to isolate (with a lot of effort) just a few mg of somatostatin. In November, 1977, the Genentech Corp. made a somatostatin analog (in the bacterium Escherichia coli) to the human hormone by introduc-ing the synthetic gene in a transporter (plasmid) and by coupling this gene with that of the large protein beta-galactosidase. As the researchers at Genentech found out, somatostatin does not contain the amino acid methionine.

This amino acid, when it exists in protein chains, is easily cut by the chemically reactant cyanogen-bromide. Therefore, it is possible to attach somatos-tatin to the large protein using methionine. It pre-vents the little peptide from being damaged by bacteria, and makes it easier to separate from the protein beta-galactosidase with cyanogen bromide, as is illustrated in the diagram below.

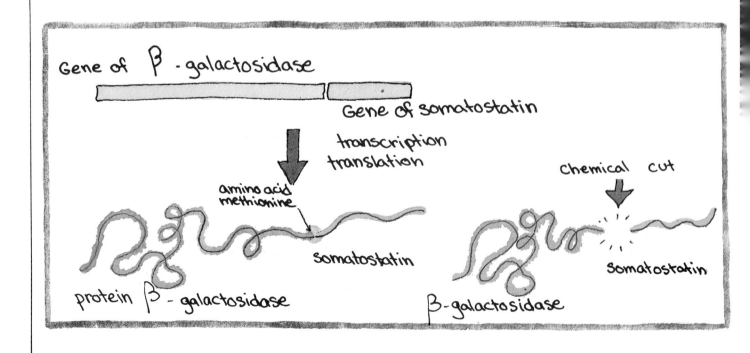

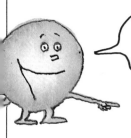

If you want to make more proteins, here are some interesting sequences:

▶ Glucagon: His Ser Glu Gly Thr Phe Thr Ser Asp Tyr Ser Lys Tyr Leu Asp

▶ LRF, a brain hormone: Glu His Trp Ser Tyr Gly Leu Arg Pro Gly

▶ vasopresin: Cys Tyr Phe Gln Asn Cys Pro Arg Gly

▶ angiotensin: Asp Arg Val Tyr Ile His Pro Phe

But if you want to make a molecule of human albumin, good luck! It has 1052 amino acids!

Here are some applications of the Biokit

The Biokit allows the illustration of a certain number of processes or biological techniques that have recently been discovered. These discoveries have played an important role in the development of modern biology.

1. mutations
2. the gene-making machine
3. fishing for genes
4. genetic engineering

1. Mutations: changes in the code

A mutation is a local change in the genetic code carried by the DNA, such as the replacement, erasure or modification of one or many "letters" of the code. These "minting" errors, or errors in the copying of the genetic text, are due to either physical causes (ultra violet light, for example) or chemical causes (mutagens). The changing of the genetic information induces, in turn, a change in the structure of the corresponding proteins. Their function can be disturbed, and diseases and weaknesses may result.

An interesting example allows us to illustrate the effect of a mutation causing a serious blood disease, sickle-cell anemia, in which abnormal red blood cells are formed in a sickle shape. This disease affects millions of people in Africa.

This different shape of the red blood cells is caused by a modification of the hemoglobin, the protein that carries the red pigment of the blood, and links up with oxygen. These modified molecules attach to one another and form long fibers that deform the red blood cell and cause the disease. These deformed red blood cells block the blood vessels.

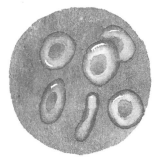
Normal red blood cells

Sickle-shaped red blood cells

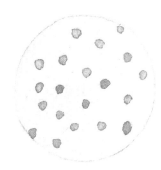
Normal hemoglobin

Hemoglobin found in sickle-cell anemia

What's the reason for this molecular change? Simply a chemically-perturbed grouping that instructs the molecules to link up to one another improperly.

 Normal hemo-globin chemical modification abnormal hemoglobin →

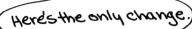
Here's the only change.

To understand the importance of such a mutation and the life threatening disease that results from it, take the Biokit and make the section of normal protein, and the section of modified protein.

This modified hemoglobin is the result of one single change in the protein chain: the replacement of glutamic acid by valine.

- Normal hemoglobin chain

HEM A   VAL - HIS - LEU - THR - PRO - GLU - GLU - LYS
          1   2   3   4   5   6   7   8

- Modified hemoglobin chain (after mutation)

HEM B   VAL - HIS - LEU - THR - PRO - VAL - GLU - LYS
          1   2   3   4   5   6   7   8

Something has happened in the genetic code, more precisely in the codon which codes for the amino acid glutamin. This codon has been mutated.

Normal sequence (hemoglobin A)

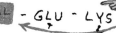

G U A C A U U U A A C U C C U G A A G A A A A A
Val His Leu Thr Pro Glu Glu Lys

⇓

modified sequence (hemoglobin B).

G U A C A U U U A A C U C C U G U A G A A A A A
Val His Leu Thr Pro Val Glu Lys

First, make the code corresponding to the normal hemoglobin sequence. Then simply replace the A in the codon GAA (that codes for glutamic acid) with a U. This gives GUA which codes for valine. This single simple change creates a fearsome hereditary disease that affects millions of people.

2. The Lifewriting Machine

For the past several years, the synthesis of nucleic acids has been a topic of considerable importance. Today one can, in effect, chemically write the language of life, composing letter by letter the genetic code for a given protein, and introducing this artificial gene into a microorganism or into a cell where it will express itself. These chemical syntheses are difficult to do by hand as they are long, repetitive and tedious.

This is why researchers directed their attention toward devising an automated machine with microprocessors capable of carrying out one by one the chemical reactions necessary for synthesis of a gene. Such machines are now commercially available.

The researcher types in the genetic code of the protein he wants to synthesize.

The machine attaches the "letters" of the genetic code one to another and in the indicated order.

After several hours, the machine produces a fragment of artificial gene.

When you have used the Biokit to make your first copy of a gene, you've done something similar to what the life-writing machine does: attach, letter by letter, the elements forming the genetic code untill construction of a complete plan is introduced into a microorganism to direct the synthesis of a protein.

The difference is that the machines make double stranded DNA (the T in place of the U, and deoxyribose in place of ribose) while you've made the messenger RNA.

Train yourself (it will be of use to you later) to make the sequence. This little sequence is about to help you "fish" for molecules of messenger RNA that will help make a working gene. The sequence is AGGUUUCAA.

One of the first machines to synthesize genes, first available commercially in 1981.

3. To isolate a gene: "Fishing for RNA"

Biologists today know how to transcribe a single-stranded RNA in the double-stranded DNA, that is, in a functioning gene. That's why this DNA is called complementary.

One uses an enzyme that copies RNA to DNA, Reverse Transcriptase. But for that one needs a natural messenger RNA. How can it be isolated among the thousands of different molecules of messenger RNA always being created by the cell? A very clever technique provides an answer to that question: "Fishing for RNA" using a radioactive probe capable of circling the wanted molecule, "tying it up" and isolating it from the rest of the molecules. Here is the principle it's based on.

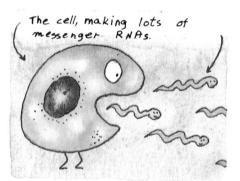

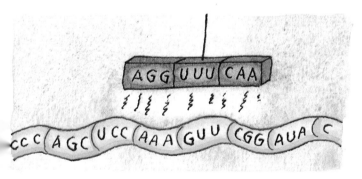

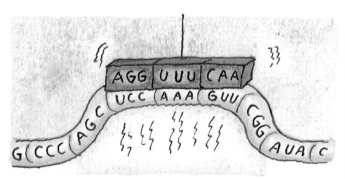

Thanks to the Biokit, you, too, are going to isolate an RNA molecule from many others. You have just made a probe: A G G U U U C A A. Take this probe and put a small label on it on which you're going to write "danger: radioactive isotope." Next, make the following sequence:

AAC CAG CCU AGC UUU UCC AAA GUU CCA GUU AGC

Now gently slide your probe over the messenger RNA. You realize that **only one sequence can attach to your probe**, and that's the sequence U C C A A A G U U. Your molecule of messenger RNA is now "marked" by radioactivity. It will become possible to sort it out from those thousands of others.

When you have isolated the messenger RNA how can you recopy it into the complementary DNA? Here's the technique that allows us to do this, illustrated by the following drawing:

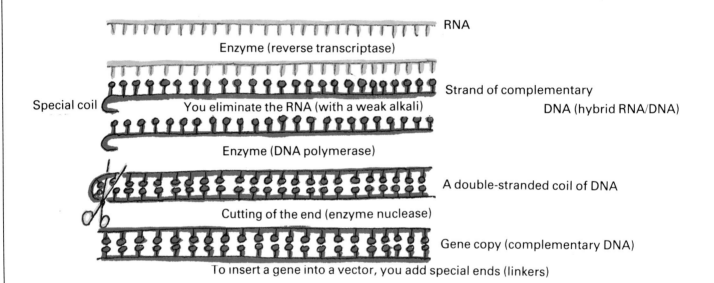

RNA

Enzyme (reverse transcriptase)

Special coil

Strand of complementary DNA (hybrid RNA/DNA)

You eliminate the RNA (with a weak alkali)

Enzyme (DNA polymerase)

A double-stranded coil of DNA

Cutting of the end (enzyme nuclease)

Gene copy (complementary DNA)

To insert a gene into a vector, you add special ends (linkers)

4. Genetic Engineering: Molecular programming

Now, consider an artificial or isolated gene. The gene is a program of assembly instructions. It can supervise the building of the cellular factory (bacteria or higher cells) and make it produce the protein that the scientist is looking for: insulin, interferon, growth hormone or antigen for the production of a vaccine.

How does this gene get into the cell whose protein synthesis machine it is supervising? First of all, it is attached to the inside of a transport DNA molecule called a vector (a small ring of DNA, a plasmid, of which there are about 20–30 copies in a bacterial cell). Plasmids are produced today by biologists, and contain well-defined sequences for start, stop, amplification, recognition signals, etc. On the next page, on the left, is the chart of a perfect genetic engineer.

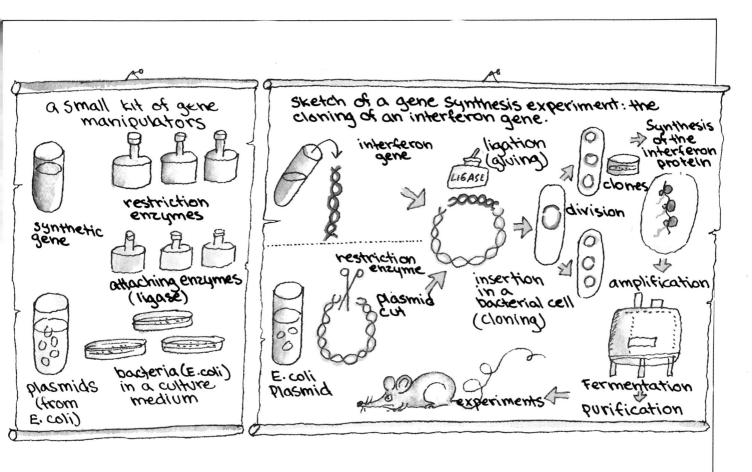

With the Biokit, you're going to illustrate one of the most important aspects of genetic engineering: the cutting of the genes by the restriction enzymes, and the attaching of them with the help of the enzyme ligase.

1. Take two strips of cardboard and assemble the following sequence, not forgetting to replace U by T, since we're working with DNA, not RNA.

In the sequence that you've made, look for the sequence GAATTC. It's exactly the sequence that is recognized by one of the more frequently used restriction enzymes, the enzyme Eco R1. This enzyme attaches itself to that sequence, and cuts the DNA in there.

2. With scissors (representing the enzyme Eco R1) cut the cardboard strip between the base G and the base A, and between bases A and G, as indicated on the drawing below. Here are the two pieces that result.

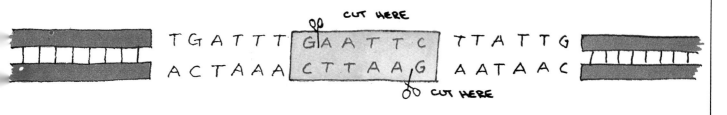

You can see that each of the two cut ends can find a complementary place to which it can be attached. These are called cohesive ends.

Change some bases of fragment no. 2, for example, and introduce any sequence you want. It's like having another gene, but one that's been cut off by the same restriction enzyme. These cohesive ends are complementary to those of fragment no. 1. They therefore put themselves in position complementary to each other. Now, nothing can interfere with the activity of the enzyme ligase which attaches the ends together – a new gene has been produced.

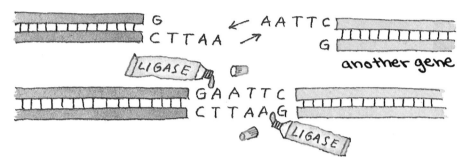

Here's how the cutting and soldering that forms the basis for the genetic engineering are done.

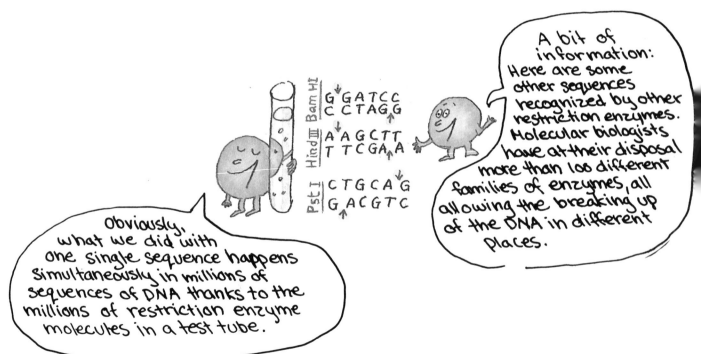

The organization of genes in cells of higher organisms

The genes of lower organisms (such as bacteria that we call procaryotes) are attached one to another. A gene in such an organism produces a messenger RNA of the same length as the gene. But in cells of higher organisms, called eucaryotes, the coding sequences for proteins are separated by untranslated zones. These coding sequences are called **exons**, and the non-coding zones, **introns**.

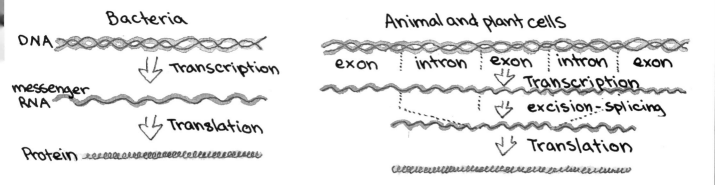

This separation of genes is very important, and allows the recombination of different fragments with one another. This increases the variety of products that can be made by the genes. With the Biokit you can make a sequence of messenger RNA as long as two cardboard strips. After that you can cut apart 30 letters of a central element, and fuse the two pieces again. In this way you have excised the fully transcribed messenger RNA and transformed it into a shorter RNA of exons only.

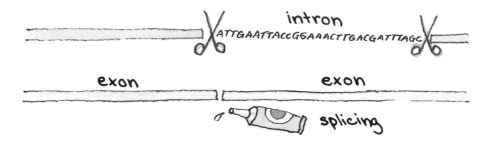

The control of the reactions of life

The processes of copying and translating start at well-defined places on the gene. The copying machine (RNA polymerase) recognizes the place on the DNA where it must start its transcription of the DNA into RNA (this particular sequence is called the promoter).

The switch for the copying machine, the "repressor," recognizes its place on the DNA. Finally, the ribosome (the translating machine) recognizes its place on the messenger RNA. In addition to all these signals to start, this molecular mechanism can stop itself in two ways (like F. Jacob and J. Monod showed for the bacteria).

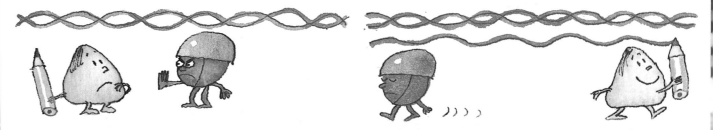

If the repressor is present on the DNA, fixed on the operator gene, the DNA cannot be copied. Above, a first explanation of the mechanism that stops the copying from the DNA to the messenger RNA.

Above, copying is possible. The repressor is absent. It is detached from the gene operator. The enzyme RNA polymerase can do its work.

In inductable or repressable systems in which a repressor molecule can be attached to and detached from the DNA, there are small molecules that are also recognized by the repressor. If these small molecules (made by the enzymes) working "at the assembly line" accumulate in too great a quantity, two mechanisms intervene:

The first, below, blocks the first enzyme of the chain, and the whole synthesis stops. The enzymes reassess the situation as soon as the number of small molecules goes down.

The second, below, reinforces the linkage of the repressor of the DNA, thereby blocking the enzymes' messenger RNA synthesis and dismantling the assembly line.

This journey through life's control center is now finished. Protix and the author hope you continue your interest in biology, one of the sciences that will very probably mark the twenty-first century, which is almos upon us.